The VOICE of FAITH

Whosoever Can Have Whatsoever They Say!

CYNTHIA BRAZELTON

The VOICE of FAITH

Whosoever Can Have Whatsoever They Say!

CONTENTS

DEDICATION 9

FORWARD 11

ACKNOWLEDGEMENTS 13

PREFACE 14

INTRODUCTION 15

CHAPTER 1 | THE FIGHT 19

RELEASE YOUR FAITH 25

CHAPTER 2 | COURAGEOUS FAITH 31

RELEASE YOUR FAITH 35

CHAPTER 3 | HIS NEED 43

RELEASE YOUR FAITH 46

CHAPTER 4 | YOU CAN HAVE WHATSOEVER 53

RELEASE YOUR FAITH 61

CHAPTER 5 | BELIEVE YOU RECEIVE 69

RELEASE YOUR FAITH 74

ABOUT THE AUTHOR   81

CONTACT   84

DEDICATION

Many years ago, I had a dream that I was in labor about to give birth. I was rushed to the hospital only to find myself standing in the hallway of the hospital bent over. My baby was coming so fast that I couldn't make it to the delivery room. I was calling for a doctor to come and help, but still ended up giving birth right in the hallway. What was strange about the birth was when I delivered, the baby was still in its amniotic sac. I could see, very clearly, every feature of the baby, even the fact, that the umbilical cord was still attached to me.

The baby was beautiful! I could see the baby moving as if it was fighting, trying to get out of the sac. Finally, I was taken to my room (still holding the baby), I began to notice that there were a lot of people around me admiring the child saying things like, "Oh my, what a beautiful baby." "I've never seen a baby so beautiful." They commented on physical details like the hair, eyes and skin. As I looked down to see my baby, the imaged changed to books. There were a whole lot of books in my arms. The people around me were now saying, "Oh what a wonderful book; that helped me a lot." "That was so powerful; it changed my life." And then, I woke up.

In light of this dream, I dedicate this book and those to come, to my God who has blessed me with many wonderful dreams and visions.

To my Lord and Savior Jesus Christ who taught me how to live and walk by faith. It is because of the faithfulness of Jesus who died for me and loves me, I live. To the Holy Spirit, who is my teacher, my guide, and my friend, who reveals to me heavenly realities.

Cynthia Brazetton

FOREWORD

I have been with my beautiful wife, Cynthia for over 35 years. To be married to a woman of faith who loves God, loves His Word, loves me and believes in me is absolutely priceless. It has been a blessing to stand together in faith for the will of God for our lives. Throughout the years, we have seen a multitude of supernatural manifestations that cover the whole human experience; salvations, healings, deliverances, prosperity in the face of impossible odds, troubles, and persecutions of all kinds. Together we have learned we can do all things through Christ. His faith and His faith alone has made all this possible.

Galatians 2:16 (New King James Version) says, "Knowing that a man is not justified by the works of the law, BUT by THE FAITH OF JESUS Christ, EVEN WE HAVE BELIEVED in Jesus Christ, that we might be justified by the faith of Christ, and not by the works of the law: for by the works of the law shall no flesh be justified."

I want you to pay attention to the words "even we have believed." Understand our belief is in the faith or faithfulness of Jesus Christ. It is His faithfulness that has caused all these experiences to turn out for our good. Hebrews 11:6 tells us that without faith it is impossible to please God, but he that comes to God must believe that He is. Faith for me is more than just believing God for something, it is a relationship of trust. Trusting that He is the source of whatever He has planned for our lives.

Your faith in God should be seen and heard. You are a product of what you believe, and you'll know what you believe by what's coming out of your mouth. Put the word of God in your mouth and speak to your circumstances. In this book, *The Voice of Faith*, you will learn the word of God that's available to you, how to access it, and how to unlock the wisdom you need to manifest all the promises of God. Get ready to believe and receive!

Apostle Tony Brazelton

ACKNOWLEDGEMENTS

There are so many wonderful people the Lord has placed in my life who have been a source of strength and encouragement to do what God has put in my heart to do. For that, I am eternally grateful.

To my wonderful husband Tony Brazelton who in every venture of our lives has not wavered in your stance to see what God said come to pass. You are a great man of faith.

To my children Tony Jr., Antoinette, Jordan, and Aaron, thank you for never doubting us but always standing in faith with your parents; your love for God and me has been immeasurable.

To our spiritual parents, Pastors Creflo and Taffi Dollar, thank you for your belief in us and your support in our journey of faith.

To all of my dear friends who are always encouraging me to put that sermon into a book, Thank You.

To all the members and partners of Victory Christian Ministries Intl. and TCBM Sons and Daughters,
thank you for your continued love and support.

Many thanks to the midwives that helped me birth this book.

PREFACE

God has a master plan for our lives. It is through our time spent with Him, receiving what Jesus did and being led by the Holy Spirit, that we begin to discover that plan.

God has given us His word to help us to walk it out. In the parable of the sower found in Matthew 13, Mark 4, and Luke 8, the seed is the word of God and the ground is man's heart. God wants to put His word in your heart so you can be changed into the same.

Any time we can see the word, hear the word, and understand the word, that's the time we can be changed into that word we see, hear, and understand.

INTRODUCTION

A WORD FROM CYNTHIA BRAZELTON

In life's journey, it is important that we know our basic human rights as these rights enhance our lives. For example, naturally we have the right to life and liberty without discrimination. Spiritually we have the same rights, however, many live without exercising their rights. In the same token, Faith has been given to you without discrimination. We have the right to release our faith because every person has been given the measure of faith. So why aren't we using it?

I had someone recently come to me seeking answers to the hardship they were facing at the time. They had borrowed all they could have borrowed and believed as much as they could; however, they were still wondering how and why they were in the same situation. I began to remind them of who they were and of their rights as a believer.

Mark 11:23 states, *"For verily I say unto you, That whosoever shall say unto this mountain, Be thou removed, and be thou cast into the sea; and shall not doubt in his heart, but shall believe that those things which he saith shall come to pass; he shall have whatsoever he saith."* Well you and I are a *Whosoever* and we can have

Whatsoever we say. We have to say the right things as we release our faith for manifestation.

According to Romans 12:3-6, *"God has dealt to every man the measure of faith."* There is no lack of faith and there is a grace for every area of our lives to prosper. Ultimately, we have the faith for the grace to prosper. We simply must use our words to bring into manifestation what God has already provided.

Chapter 1

THE FIGHT

In this book, I want to dispel the lies the devil has established, so that you can see the manifestation of what God said in His word belongs to you. God has given many promises concerning our personal blessings. Having this knowledge as a foundational truth may require a moment of determination that stimulates you to fight for what you know and understand is your promise. Because God has already provided all things, we have the confidence to engage in the pursuit of all that is promised.

Sometimes we become passive when it comes to the things that God has for us, and we allow the circumstances of life to dictate to us whether we can have something or not. But God has a bigger plan than that. God has already set you up to win.

You already have the victory! However, there are times when you will have to fight and pursue all that God has for you. During those periods, you cannot sit around and wait for things to happen. You must begin to speak the Word of God concerning all things in order to walk in the revelation of His promises.

God did not create us to be defeated in any area of our lives. His desire is to supply our needs and wants in every area that affects us personally. Understanding His desire for you will cause another level of activation in your faith. But remember when you are challenged in this area, it is not God who is causing your pain. It is not in God's nature *(temperament, personality or character)* to allow bad things to happen to you to teach you anything. It is the goodness of God that causes you to have a remorseful and moldable heart. His enjoyment is in being good to you. He would never take anything from you.

You may have needs and desires that you want God to manifest in your life, yet your habit is to investigate natural methods for the answer to those needs, while forgetting what the Lord has already spoken through His Word. Understanding His word is an essential element in seeing the manifestation of His promise. In Matthew 6:33, it tells you to *seek first the kingdom of heaven and all His righteousness and all these things will be added unto you.* This means that God is not leaving anything out. Everything you need and everything He has for you will be provided.

The truth is you have an enemy out there and this enemy is not playing fair. His ultimate goal is to take everything from you. The scripture states in John 10:10, *"The thief cometh not, but for to steal, and to kill, and to destroy; I am come that they might have life, and that they might have it more abundantly."*

As you can see, it is the devil that comes to steal, kill and destroy, and it is Jesus who came that you may have life and life more abundantly that overflows from its fullness. This is the total opposite of lack. Therefore, when you are experiencing lack, it is not God's will.

His plans for your life promise the abundance to operate (Ephesians 3:20) exceedingly, above all that you could ask or think according to a power that works in you, and this power is according to His riches in glory by Christ Jesus. Philippians 4:19 states: *"But my God shall supply all your need according to his riches in glory by Christ Jesus."*

It is not His will that you lack in any area of your life. It doesn't matter if it is your health, family or finances; God has already supplied everything you will need to be successful. You do not have to wait to experience another report concerning deficits; you are in your season of suddenly! Something is about to happen for you, and it will be a sudden occurrence!

Once you understand that God will supply all your needs according to His riches in glory, you have to say this to yourself on a regular basis. Speak to yourself what the Word of God proclaims, especially when your need is talking back to you, saying what you cannot have. *"My God shall supply all of my needs"* is a promise that cannot and will not be changed.

Not only are there supplies that God will provide from His heavenly resources, but there are also resources that are tagged with your name on it. Pursue what God says belongs to you with the words of your mouth. However, *your words must match the promise*. Meaning, you cannot talk defeat and expect the victory to manifest.

The Bible says, *"Let the weak say I am strong"* (Joel 3:10). When the enemy begins to talk nonsense, you must talk back with the Word of the Lord and walk out the victory. This means you can't sit or stand still. You keep walking even when you don't see the manifestation of what is promised, and all the promises of God will catch up with you. Don't ever give up! Don't quit! Keep on pursuing and fighting for what God has said is yours. Your deliverance, healing and breakthrough will be expressed. It is simply your time!

Ephesians 3:20 says God can do exceedingly and abundantly above all you can ask or think according to a power that is in Christ Jesus working on the inside of you. When the devil tries to tell you it's not working based on what you can see in your circumstances, you have to grasp that you are filled with the Spirit of God which is overflowing in your life and it is working for you.

Have you ever prayed for something and it appeared to take forever to manifest? It is in these moments when the enemy will try to convince you that the power of God in you is not productive. He will say things like *"You are not going to get this house"* or *"You are not going to get that job."* Or he will say, *"You are not going to be healed."* He will even try to make you believe you are not good enough. He plays on your fears and tries to make you believe in your inadequacies. During these moments is when your voice is most powerful! You have to talk to yourself and say, *"I have a power that is working on the inside of me!"*

God is saying this is the season where the things that He has ordained for you will be manifested and you will have them suddenly. Things that appear to take a long time will begin to happen in a day's time. If you would be bold enough to believe it, you will receive it!

Declare this over your life, *I'm in my season of the suddenly!* God has supplied everything we need to be successful. There are enough resources for us all to be successful. Why not get your share? Now is the time for the harvest of the seeds you've been sowing. You've been sowing for years and then suddenly, here comes your harvest. If you're believing God for healing, you don't have to wait. Something is about to happen...and suddenly! You have to talk to yourself and say, *"My God shall supply all my needs!"*

Now is the time to recognize your season of overflow and declare that you are not looking for just enough to get by or just enough to take care of your circumstances. Proclaim that you have more than you need, for the season has arrived for the fullness in abundance.

Prophesy over yourself and get the Word of God deep inside of you. He wants you to have a life that is overflowing. Declare to the enemy that he is not going to take anything from you. Don't wait till you see it. You have to walk it out. That which God has said belongs to you; it's already yours.

RELEASE YOUR FAITH

Prophesy over yourself and get the Word of God deep inside of you.

Chapter 2

COURAGEOUS FAITH

The word *courageous* is a quality of your spirit and of your mind to face difficulty, danger, and pain without fear. It means to be brave and to have the courage of one's convictions, to act in accordance with one's beliefs, especially in spite of criticism or circumstances.

The Bible displays many who courageously released their voice of faith in the face of difficulty. Let's look at the voice of faith of a few people who took God seriously. In Matthew chapter 9, there were a series of events going on that day that will test their convictions.

Jairus, the ruler of the synagogue, has a daughter at home who is at the point of death. He came to see Jesus with a voice of faith saying, *"If you will come to my house and lay your hands on my daughter, she will be healed."* Jesus said, *"I will come."* Being a ruler, I would imagine he never traveled alone and had many men with him. Jesus also never traveled alone. We know he had at least the 12 disciples with him. Anytime Jesus was around, the crowd would grow. Wanting to see the miracle that was about to take place, the crowd followed him. You can imagine the buzz of the crowd saying things like, *"Jesus is with Jairus and He is about to heal his daughter."*

On the way to Jairus' house, with an ever-growing crowd following, a woman who had an issue of blood heard Jesus was near. She had been suffering for 12 years with no end in sight. Picture her leaving the doctor's office when she ran into the crowd. There are whispers echoing through the crowd that Jesus is going to heal Jairus's daughter. Then she said within herself, *"If I could just touch the hem of His garment, I will be healed."* That is the voice of faith. She PRESSED her way to Jesus. You know you are convinced because you are PRESSED.

The moment she touched the hem of His garment, immediately she knew within herself she was made whole. Jesus immediately knowing that virtue had left Him asked, *"WHO TOUCHED ME?"* C'mon Jesus, the disciples probably thought, with this big crowd, there are many people touching you. The Bible says He turned to see HER. He knew who touched Him. You have to ask yourself, have you been so pressed that you are really touching Jesus? Is He turning to see YOU? The woman with fear and trembling told Jesus her testimony and said, *"I've gone to many physicians and spent all that I had and never got any better, only grew worse. I knew if I could just touch you, I could be made whole."* He said, *"Daughter, YOUR FAITH has made you whole, go in peace and be whole."* This woman received physical healing as well as total restoration.

While Jesus was speaking to the woman here comes one of Jairus' servants saying, *"No need to trouble the Master, your daughter has died."* I'm sure the entire crowd heard that. Jesus arrested that thought and told Jairus, *"Be not afraid, only believe."*

Jesus continues on to Jairus' house; the scene was horrifying. People were crying at the death of this little girl. Jesus says, *"She's not dead, she is only sleeping."* That is the voice of faith. The same crowd that was crying were now laughing Jesus to scorn. Jesus put them all out! Sometimes you have to put the people out that don't believe like you do.

He told the girl to get up and she got up. The testimony of both accounts rippled throughout the crowd. They were astonished. So astonished that in that same crowd two blind men were now catching on that you have to have the voice of faith. They wanted to seize the opportunity for themselves, so they followed behind Jesus. They were so courageous they went right into the house where Jesus was and cried out, *"Jesus, Son of David, have mercy on us."* Jesus said to them, *"Do you believe I am able to do this?"* They responded, *"Yes Lord, we do."* He then touched their eyes and said, *"Become what you believe."*

In the book of Matthew there were two other men having the same issue. They were also blind, and they cried out, *"Jesus, thou son of David, have mercy on us!"* Can you imagine that crowd telling them to shut up and be quiet? But their position was no one else knew what it was like to be blind, so they cried out the more. Jesus asked them, *"What do you want from me?"* They asked for their eyes to be opened. Jesus touched their eyes and immediately they had their sight.

People would love for you to keep your mouth shut; they will tell you to be quiet, but only you know what you need! And when you are convinced, and when you believe, you will cry out, you will press through, and you will become what you believe.

RELEASE YOUR FAITH

And when you are convinced, and when you believe, you will cry out, you will press through, and you will become what you believe.

_____

_____

_____

_____

_____

_____

_____

_____

_____

_____

_____

_____

_____

_____

_____

_____

_____

_____

_____

Chapter 3

HIS NEED

In Mark 11 beginning with verse 12, we read that Jesus is hungry and has a need for food. The way Jesus handles His need is the same way you should handle yours. Every time there was a need in His life, He knew there was a supply for it. We declare that as Jesus is so are we in this world, so we should walk it out. Begin to speak this out loud to get it in your spirit: "*There is a supply for every need in my life!*"

That's one you ought to put on your refrigerator. You need to say it every time a need arises and watch what happens. Go after what God says is yours. If you continue in the Word of God, it will manifest for you.

Let's go back to the scripture. In Mark 11:13 it says Jesus was hungry and He saw a fig tree afar off. He was happy the fig tree had leaves, assuming there would be fruit on the tree to eat. Have you ever had a need in your life, and you thought about who or what could help you with it, especially since they had the resources to do it, and you got there, and they told you no?

Jesus gets to the fig tree and sees that it has no fruit. Because of this, Jesus answered the fig tree and says, *"No man will eat from you again."* Once Jesus spoke to the tree, it withered up immediately from the root. The moment Jesus spoke, *immediately* something happened.

This concept is one I would like for you to truly understand. Jesus didn't hope or wish. He spoke and it happened. You have the same authority. The moment you open your mouth to speak, *immediately* things begin to happen. Jesus went on with His day.

The next morning as they passed by, they saw the fig tree dried up from the roots. Peter called to remembrance what Jesus said, *"Master, behold, the fig tree you cursed is withered away."* Like Peter, there are times in your life you have to remember what God said. The disciples were amazed, and Jesus said to them, (verse 22) *"Have faith in God"* or have the faith of God. I don't know what you've been going through but have faith in God.

God is faithful, reliable and dependable. You can count on Him. This is the power behind your proclamations. In Isaiah 55 God says, *"and so shall my word be."* The Word of God must become *your* word.

Isaiah 55:10-11 says, *"For as the rain cometh down, and the snow from heaven, and returneth not thither, but watereth the earth, and maketh it bring forth and bud, that it may give seed to the sower, and bread to the eater: So shall my word be that goeth forth out of my mouth: it shall not return unto me void, but it shall accomplish that which I please, and it shall prosper in the thing whereto I sent it."*

So, shall it be for *you*. The words that you speak shall not come back void or empty; they will accomplish what they have been sent to do. They will do exactly what you have said, but you must say what you mean and mean what you say.

Be faithful to the word that you have spoken out of your heart but be careful not to go back to speaking your circumstances. I know that this may appear to be hard, especially when you want people to understand what is going on in your life. However, you must be very careful concerning what you are saying. Remember, we don't focus on the circumstance, we focus on the Word of God.

RELEASE YOUR FAITH

Be faithful to the word that you have spoken out of your heart but be careful not to go back to speaking your circumstances.

_____

_____

_____

_____

_____

_____

_____

_____

_____

_____

_____

_____

_____

_____

_____

_____

_____

_____

_____

_____

Chapter 4

YOU CAN HAVE WHATSOEVER

Mark 11:23 says this, *"For verily I say unto you, that whosoever shall say unto this mountain, Be thou removed, and be thou cast into the sea; and shall not doubt in his heart, but shall believe that those things which he saith shall come to pass; he shall have whatsoever he saith."*[Emphasis added].

If you are a *"whosoever"* you've got to say something. You get into situations where you don't have enough, or you have a desire that is unfulfilled, but you aren't saying anything and if you're not saying anything, you won't have anything. Poverty is the enemy of a believer. God didn't call us to be beggars. You're not a beggar, you're a *whosoever*. You have to speak to poverty, speak to your lack! Your prosperity is one word away. Don't wait to exercise your right to speak to poverty. Do it now!

I speak generational blessing into your house, into your life. In everything as people of God we are blessed. Poverty is what's holding you back from achieving what God has for you, but money isn't your holdup, *your mouth* is what's holding you back. Declare *"I am rich. I am a whosoever!"*

You are a *whosoever*, you can have *whatsoever* you say, so say it. Say what your whatsoever is. Just like Jesus you can speak to it and it shall obey you.

There are times when the enemy will try to disqualify you based on who you are and your circumstances, but the Word of the Lord is clear; it states that *"whosoever…"* This word is not defined by your condition, title or your status but is a broad stroke covering all those who believe. You are the *whosoever!* It is so important for you to know that the *whosoever* is whoever has faith in God. Declare this over your life *"I'm a whosoever! I have whatsoever! I have everything I need. Poverty, you don't belong here. Wealth and riches shall be in my house."* Say *'I'm a whosoever and I have whatsoever!"* The whosoever can speak, and it shall be done!

The only qualification to manifest this type of faith is to be a *whosoever!* All doubt must be removed from your heart. You cannot be double minded about what you say. In the same way that Jesus spoke to the fig tree, you have the authority to speak to your circumstance and have your words manifest. In doing this, your confession will match your testimony and say, *"It came to past".*

I don't know what your mountain is today, but you have the authority to talk to it. You are a *whosoever* who can do this. Once you speak to the condition, let it know that you are the *whosoever* who can have *whatsoever* you say. No longer will the conditions or circumstances (mountains) of your life have permission to dictate the outcome or the process, but you will take the authority that is in Christ Jesus who lives in you and speak!

Those mountains will get out of your way, they will be removed and cast into the sea. The obstructions that appear too great, will *be thou removed.* The lack in your life will *be thou removed.* The sickness in your life will *be thou removed.* Declare this out loud "*I am sending my word and it shall be as I have said!*"

You must believe that you are the "whosever" who can have "whatsoever" you say if there is no doubt in your heart. God is very specific concerning these things and so must you be. Don't just accept what comes to you; be precise in what you believe, and it will manifest.

The Word of God does not say you can have a "whatever," it says you can have "whatsoever." Be specific and strategically target your words to pursue what you say. The enemy would like for you to accept "whatever" because it is not specific to your needs, but God stated that you can state the "whatsoever" and receive it according to your faith.

You should never settle for "whatever!" Your needs are distinctive, and so should your words be that are trained to bring into fruition your desired outcome. Get your "whatsoever!" Don't allow anyone to have you settle for less than what is promised. Being a "whosoever" who believes God and can speak to mountains, will always demand and have "whatsoever" he or she says, so never settle.

Matthew 21:21 *"Jesus answered and said unto them, Verily I say unto you, If ye have faith, and doubt not, ye shall not only do this which is done to the fig tree, but also if ye shall say unto this mountain, Be thou removed, and be thou cast into the sea; it shall be done."* Here are a few examples of how we put this Word into practice:

He's the God of the Toothpaste!

I recently had a pastor drop off toothpaste at my house. I thought, That's different. Of all the things you would bring to someone's home, toothpaste? Later that evening my daughter came to me and I asked if I had toothpaste because she ran out.

Typically, you don't run out of toothpaste, but she uses a special brand and had given hers away earlier. I said to her, *"You know, I thought it was strange, but someone brought me toothpaste earlier."* Her same brand. She gave God praise. Before she asked, God already supplied it. He's the God of the toothpaste! Not only that, He's the God of the toilet paper! Read on.

He's the God of the Toilet Paper!

I can remember in the first few years of our marriage, Tony and I made a decision to trust God for everything. I do mean everything. There was a time where we ran out of toilet paper. That's one of Tony's pet peeves, never run out of toilet paper, but we did.

I told him that we only had five dollars in the bank and if we take that out, it may close the account. We didn't want to do that, so we did what we know how to do, we prayed for toilet paper. We prayed a simple yet very sincere prayer. *"Father we know that you supply our every need, so we thank you for supplying toilet paper."*

Suddenly there was a knock at the door. A friend of ours came to tell us about a job she just got at Proctor and Gamble. She had samples of products and asked could we use some *TOILET PAPER* and presented us with a case of toilet paper. Praise God! God cares about everything concerning you and there is a divine supply for every area of your life!

He is the God of the Jet!

On September 11, 2001 we all know what happened. It changed the way we would be able to travel. My husband's and my travel schedules were only increasing, and the Lord spoke to us and told us to ask Him for a jet of our own. At that time, we did not know much about jets. We began researching how to buy a jet and what type of jet we would need. We began to work with a jet broker. He gave us a great deal. While we were working out a deal with him, the Lord spoke to my husband and said that someone was going to give us a jet. *Give* us a jet. We said what the Lord said and told the man someone would give us a jet. He laughed and even said, *"No one will give you a jet."*

Some time passed and we were in Florida attending a conference where our spiritual father Dr. Creflo Dollar was ministering. During offering time, my husband and I decided to sow the largest seed to date for the Jet God promised us. As we were walking back to our seats, a man of God walked over to us and told us, *"God has been dealing with me all day about giving you my plane."* Once his words fully registered, I was so excited about the new plane praising God and I looked at my husband who didn't say a word. In that moment the Lord spoke to him and said, *"Keep believing me for a jet."* While we were thankful for the plane, we knew in our hearts God specifically said to us a Jet. This plane would still be a tremendous blessing to us to meet our travel needs at that time. But we knew our whatsoever was a Jet. Don't ever despise small beginnings and also be careful not to settle for whatever. The plane given to us was seed that we would eventually give away and receive a harvest. We were blessed to fly our own private plane. It was our first but would not be our last aircraft. The story continues.

Two months passed and we continued to do what we always do: We believed God and sow our seeds with thanksgiving. Remembering what God has said to you and how God has blessed you in the past helps to build your faith. We had a word from God that someone would give us a jet. We stood on that word, we confessed that word and soon after, that word manifested.

Flying down to Atlanta for a speaking engagement we got a call from Dr. Dollar to meet at his hangar. He showed us a beautiful jet he had purchased and asked if we liked it. *"Do we like it? Of course, it was great!"* He said, *"Well it's yours!"* He told us that God asked him to do Him a favor. The favor was to purchase a jet for us. He gave us our new jet that day. Hallelujah! We are *whosoevers* that have been given two aircrafts! And this is not the end of the story.

Years have passed; the second aircraft needed an engine. It was either get another jet or get new engines. We often quote Revelation 19:10 which says the testimony of Jesus is the spirit of prophecy. We learned to prophesy to our situation by simply giving testimony to what He already has done. The word remember means to make real in the present what has happened in the past. We remembered and declared, *"If He did it once, He can do it again!"* It didn't manifest right away. It's important to stay in faith while you are waiting. It came to the 11th hour and it wasn't an option; we needed another jet now!

God is so faithful that He'll give you word to stand on until your manifestation. Jeremiah 1:12 tells us that *He is alert and active, watching over His word to perform it.* He gave me a word found in 2 Kings, chapter 3. It's the story of Jehoram, the king of Israel who wanted to go out and fight against the Moabites. He asked Jehoshaphat, king of Judah to fight with him. They both went out with the king of Edom to battle. They went by the way of the wilderness, and seven days in the wilderness they ran out of water. Jehoram thought God brought them out there to kill them. Jehoshaphat looked to hear from God. Someone told them that the prophet Elisha, who was known for pouring water over the hands of Elijah, was near. They all went to him and he was surprised to see Jehoram and wanted to send him away because he was wicked, but out of respect for Jehoshaphat, he instead called for the minstrels and they began to play. Elisha prophesied and instructed them to dig ditches in the whole valley. He said, *"Make this valley full of ditches, you won't see wind and you won't see rain, but your ditch will be full of water and this a light thing in the sight of the Lord."* I heard the Lord say, *"Don't worry about when, where or how it's going to happen. Dig a ditch."* Our digging was with sowing and releasing our voice of faith with praise and thanksgiving for what we believe He already provided. That same week a corporation called our ministry and expressed that they would like to "donate" a jet to our ministry. This was now the third aircraft that was given to us.

You may be reading this and thinking *"Wow"* however, speaking to the fig tree is no different than speaking to the mountain. It took the same faith for the toilet paper as it did for the jet. I was just as thankful for the toilet as I was for the jet. You must believe in what you say and then know that what you have believed will come to pass. Remember to be thankful!

Understand that this works in the negative as well as the positive; meaning you can believe you will catch that cold everybody in your office has and it will come to pass. Whatever you believe will be manifested. The limitations have been erased through this principle. Because of this, no one can determine what your *"whatsoever"* is but you.

RELEASE YOUR FAITH

He's the God of the Toilet Paper!

_____

_____

_____

_____

_____

_____

_____

_____

_____

_____

_____

_____

_____

_____

_____

_____

_____

_____

_____

_____

_____

Chapter 5

BELIEVE YOU RECEIVE

After Jesus teaches the disciples concerning this principle, He then backs it up by saying, *"Therefore, I say unto you that whatsoever things you desire when you pray and say, believe and you shall receive it."* Listen, you are not waiting in the future for something to happen, your suddenly is now. So, once you speak, it happens in the now. Don't be moved by what you see or don't see because you are living in the now moment and that which you have spoken has come into existence.

The old religious views on how things become manifested are not effective because in the spirit realm, the action has already taken place and the outcome is already completed. Re-program your thought process. Speak and believe that there is an immediate change. The fig tree appeared from the naked eye to not have changed once Jesus cursed it. But what wasn't seen was the immediate course of action that began from the root and stimulated the evidence at that very moment.

The circumstances in your life may look the same. Jesus was still hungry after cursing the tree. His need was still there, however, it wasn't until the next day that they saw what really happened in the moment that Jesus spoke. Never assume that things haven't changed. At the very moment your words meet with the target, maximum impact is immediate.

Listen, you have to have what you say before you have what you say! Say what you have! You must get this deep in your spirit. You must shut the door to everything that is speaking to you that denies you your promise and remind it of what the Word of the Lord says.

John 15:7-8 states, *"If ye abide in me, and my words abide in you, ye shall ask what ye will, and it shall be done unto you. Herein is my Father glorified, that ye bear much fruit; so, shall ye be my disciples."* Jesus was teaching the disciples how to have God-like faith through this principle. He was providing a blueprint for how to speak concerning the promises of God. He instructed the disciples to speak the Word of the Lord and not the circumstance that may have been before them. This is how the Father will always be glorified and that is through the manifestation of His Word. This is why His desire is to see the manifestation in your life.

When you begin to realize that you are a *"whosoever,"* then you can have *"whatsoever"* by remaining in Him and staying within the will of God for your life. In order to fully grasp this concept, you have to begin to put your words toward what Jesus said is yours. If you are not speaking, nothing is happening. You have the complete ability to change the circumstances of your life by what you say out of your mouth.

In Mark 11:14-21, Jesus spoke to a fig tree and it withered and died. In Mark 4:39, He spoke to the wind and rain and there was a great calm.

In John 11:43-44, He spoke to Lazarus and he was raised from the dead. In Mark 9:25, He spoke to the demon and it came out. In Matthew 8:3, He spoke to the leper and he was made clean. Do you see the pattern? Immediately and suddenly His words were obeyed. Like Jesus, you have the ability to see what you say come to past.

Mark 5:6-13 NLT, *"When Jesus was still some distance away, the man saw him, ran to meet him, and bowed low before him. With a shriek, he screamed, "Why are you interfering with me, Jesus, Son of the Most High God? In the name of God, I beg you, don't torture me"'* For Jesus had already said to the spirit, *"Come out of the man, you evil spirit'* Then Jesus demanded, *'What is your name?'* And he replied, *'My name is Legion, because there are many of us inside this man.'* Then the evil spirits begged him again and again not to send them to some distant place. There happened to be a large herd of pigs feeding on the hillside nearby. *'Send us into those pigs,'* the spirits begged. *'Let us enter them.'* So, Jesus gave them permission. The evil spirits came out of the man and entered the pigs, and the entire herd of about 2,000 pigs plunged down the steep hillside into the lake and drowned in the water.'"*

I want you to see His voice was so powerful and full of authority that he had to give the demons "permission" to go into the lake. He gave you that same power and authority, it is the voice of faith.

Micah 6:1 says, *"Hear ye what the Lord saith: 'Arise, contend thou before the mountains and let the hills hear thy voice."* Arise means to change your posture and position and come up out of the circumstances you are wallowing in. There are times when the enemy will start with small things to discourage you, and as you continue to ignore them, one day they become big things and appear as mountains.

Every small thing coming from the enemy's camp is trying to lead to something big (mountain) in your life. In these conditions, speak and let the hills hear your voice. Speak to them before they become big things. Speak boldly! Let everything, including the small things that are in your way, hear your voice.

Psalm 103:20 says, *"Bless the Lord, ye his angels, that excel in strength, that do his commandments, heartening unto the voice of his word."* You must let heaven; earth and the angels hear your voice. Everything that can speak to you needs to hear your voice in response. In Psalm 18:44 [The Amplified Bible (AMP)] it states, "As soon as they hear me, they respond and obey me..." As soon as they hear you, they will obey you. You and I were created in the image and likeness of God. We are the only beings who have the ability to articulate in speech what we desire to see come to pass.

1 Corinthians 15:45-50; *"And so it is written, the first man Adam was made a living soul; the last Adam was made a quickening spirit. Howbeit that was not first which is spiritual, but that which is natural; and afterward that which is spiritual. The first man is of the earth, earthy: the second man is the Lord from heaven. As is the earthy, such are they also that are earthy: and as is the heavenly, such are they also that are heavenly. And as we have borne the image of the earthy, we shall also*

bear the image of the heavenly. Now this I say, brethren, that flesh and blood cannot inherit the kingdom of God; neither doth corruption inherit incorruption." Philippians chapter 3 tells us we are citizens of two worlds, the kingdom of God and this natural world. We were born into this natural world and born from above. We have been given authority in two realms. When we speak, it will obey us.

Deuteronomy 30:15 [Easy to Read Version (ERV)] states, *"Today I have given you a choice between life and death, success and disaster."* You get to choose even when your life may be the opposite of what you expected to experience, you can choose another course. Verse 19 goes on to say, *"Today I am giving you a choice of two ways. And I ask heaven and earth to be witnesses of your choice. You can choose life or death. The first choice will bring a blessing. The other choice will bring a curse. So, choose life! Then you and your children will live."*

You can speak the life of God into your circumstances no matter what they may be. Heaven and earth are the witnesses to what you choose, meaning they are commanded to release what you have selected and will give you what you say. *"Do not be deceived, God will not be mocked and whatever you sow you will reap."*

The atmosphere is waiting for you to speak and declare something. The heavens and earth already know who you are. They understand that you are a *"whosoever"* and are waiting for you to say *"whatsoever."* And when you who are a *"whosoever"* begin to say *"whatsoever,"* you will have *"whatsoever"* you say that is the voice of faith.

RELEASE YOUR FAITH

And when you who are a *"whosoever"* begin to say *"whatsoever,"* you will have *"whatsoever"* you say that is the voice of faith.

_____

_____

_____

_____

_____

_____

_____

_____

_____

_____

_____

_____

_____

_____

_____

_____

_____

_____

_____

CYNTHIA BRAZELTON

Cynthia Brazelton and her husband Tony Brazelton serve as pastors and apostles of Victory Christian Ministries International (VCMI). She is the mother of four wonderful children: Tony Jr., Antoinette, Jordan, and Aaron. Together Tony and Cynthia Brazelton oversee churches located in Maryland, Florida, Virginia, Washington DC and the United Kingdom.

Apostle Cynthia is equipped with a unique anointing to teach the Word of God and to produce understanding in the hearts of God's people. She recognizes the significance of women in the body of Christ, and the role they have in accomplishing God's plan for this generation. She is the founder of Virtuous Women's Conference International (VWCI), and she ministers to thousands of women all over the world at various conferences and events.

She believes that it is no longer good enough for believers to just read, sing, and shout about the power of God; but that they are to fully manifest the power of God in their everyday lives. She believes that anytime you can *see* the Word of God, *hear* the Word of God, and *understand* the Word of God, you can be changed into the Word you see, hear, and understand. Once you are changed you can strengthen the brethren and boldly declare...As He (Jesus) is so are we in this world. (I John 4:17)

God has also called them to help other pastors and church leaders maximize the call of God on their lives. They accomplish this through Tony and Cynthia Brazelton Ministries Sons and Daughters (TCBMSD), a fellowship composed of many ministries that have formally connected with Tony and Cynthia as their spiritual parents. TCBM Sons and Daughters focuses on strong relationships, strong fellowship and successful ministry.

Other powerful books by Cynthia Brazelton coming soon!

To find more teachings concerning faith, or other specific topics that are according to your needs, please go to the website listed below to order or download.

If this book has blessed and empowered you, please send us your testimony. We would love to hear from you.

All correspondence can be sent to:

WWW.TONYANDCYNTHIABRAZELTON.ORG

PO Box 1, Temple Hills, MD 20757

1-800-GET- TCBM